Sum of

The Code of the Extraordinary Mind

Vishen Lakhiani

Conversation Starters

By BookHabits

Please Note: This is an unofficial conversation starters guide. If you have not yet read the original work or would like to read it again, get the book here.

Copyright © 2017 by BookHabits. All Rights Reserved.
First Published in the United States of America 2017

We hope you enjoy this complementary guide from BookHabits.
Our mission is to aid readers and reading groups with quality, thought provoking material to in the discovery and discussions on some of today's favorite books.

Disclaimer / Terms of Use: Product names, logos, brands, and other trademarks featured or referred to within this publication are the property of their respective trademark holders and are not affiliated with BookHabits. The publisher and author make no representations or warranties with respect to the accuracy or completeness of these contents and disclaim all warranties such as warranties of fitness for a particular purpose. This guide is unofficial and unauthorized. It is not authorized, approved, licensed, or endorsed by the original book's author or publisher and any of their licensees or affiliates.

No part of this publication may be reproduced or retransmitted, electronic or mechanical, without the written permission of the publisher.

Tips for Using BookHabits Conversation Starters:

EVERY GOOD BOOK CONTAINS A WORLD FAR DEEPER THAN the surface of its pages. The characters and their world come alive through the words on the pages, yet the characters and its world still live on. Questions herein are designed to bring us beneath the surface of the page and invite us into the world that lives on. These questions can be used to:

- Foster a deeper understanding of the book
- Promote an atmosphere of discussion for groups
- Assist in the study of the book, either individually or corporately
- Explore unseen realms of the book as never seen before

About Us:

THROUGH YEARS OF EXPERIENCE AND FIELD EXPERTISE, from newspaper featured book clubs to local library chapters, *BookHabits* can bring your book discussion to life. Host your book party as we discuss some of today's most widely read books.

Table of Contents

Introducing *The Code of the Extraordinary Mind* 6
Discussion Questions 14
Introducing the Author 35
Fireside Questions 40
Quiz Questions 51
Quiz Answers 64
Ways to Continue Your Reading 65

Introducing *The Code of the Extraordinary Mind*

The Code of the Extraordinary Mind is the result of author Vishen Lakhiani's time spent—more than two hundred hours—interviewing some of the world's most successful people, including Elon Musk and Richard Branson, among others. He also draws from his own personal experiences as well. As the subtitle says, Lakhiani gives readers ten rules to follow to live a more successful life. He begins the book by helping readers understand the "culturescape" and how the world has shaped them.

The first rule—Transcend the Culturescape—encourages readers to question the rules of the world. Lakhiani discusses the collective rules of humanity. He says these rules make you "ordinary and safe," and encourages the reader to live an "unrestricted" life.

Lakhiani's second rule—Question the Brules which are "bullshit rules" that he says have been passed down from one generation to the next, then to the next, etc. He teaches the reader to be able to identify the "Brules" because they limit creativity and growth.

The third rule—Practice Consciousness Engineering—tells readers how to "accelerate [their] growth" by accepting or rejecting these rules. Readers will learn to "think like a hacker" and learn how their beliefs and habits shape them. Rule four—Rewrite Your Models of Reality—teaches readers to focus on choices that will help them upgrade their beliefs. Many of the beliefs that have been ingrained in you since childhood can keep you from succeeding; and rule five—Upgrade Your Systems for Living—teaches readers how to better their lives by updating their daily systems.

The sixth rule—Bend Reality—is about being able to have two different visions in your mind at the same time—you have to be able to visualize your future as well as your present. Rule seven—Live in Blissipline--focuses on discipline and bliss. The author points out that the feeling of bliss you get after realizing a big goal is often fleeting, and he recommends doing an exercise called The Reverse Gap by Dan Sullivan. The reverse gap is all of the things you have accomplished. Focusing on these things will help you celebrate how far you have come. Rule eight–Create a Vision for Your Future—helps readers learn how to choose goals that lead to long-term happiness.

In rule nine—Be Unfuckwithable—Lakhiani encourages readers to set goals that they are unwilling to compromise on—the author calls this being "unfuckwithable," meaning the only person you should rely on to reach your dreams is yourself. The two things that can make you "unfuckwithable" are setting your own goals and taking responsibility for the things in your life—meaning, no more depending on others to make things happen or blaming your circumstances. Rule ten—Embrace Your Quest—brings everything together and teaches them how to live a meaningful life.

The book also includes bonus "tools for your journey." Lakhiani teaches readers "Six-Phase," a 20-minute daily workout for the mind. There is also a section in which the author summarizes the tools and practices to help readers "live the code." The author also offers an online experience for readers.

Lakhiani wrote the book in a conversational tone, so it is an easy and enjoyable read. The author says that he used the same style in his writing the book as he does in conversing with his friends over drinks. He even includes napkin illustrations in the books, as well as openness, honesty, and transparency that you would expect from a friendly conversation.

Lakhiani purposely wrote the book in four segments, which together have a cohesive content but can stand alone as well. The author values your time and wants you to be able to focus on the things that are most important to you.

In the book, Lakhiani presents over twenty new words to the English language. He believes words are powerful and felt the new words were necessary in order to describe some of the concepts in the book. The author uses a learning model called Consciousness Engineering and he teaches the readers how to learn so that you will be better prepared when you read other personal growth books.

Lakhiani relied on many people to make this book what it is—it includes over 200 hours of interviews with worldwide leaders like Richard Branson, Peter Diamandis, and Ken Wilber. The chapters were edited by Arianna Huffington and Dean Kamen.

The book has received positive reviews from fans and critics. Dave Asprey, founder of

Bulletproof Coffee said the book "will make you question everything you thought you knew about your life." It is a *New York Times* and *USA Today* Bestseller and is a Top Ten Non-Fiction title on Audible.

Discussion Questions

"Get Ready to Enter a New World"

Tip: Begin with questions dealing with broader issues to ensure ample time for quality discussions. Read through all discussion questions before engaging.

~~~

question 1

The author spent over 200 hours interviewing some of the world's most successful people. What do you think of the people he chose to interview? Do you think they were a good representation of the point he was trying to make in the book?

~~~

~~~

question 2

Vishen Lakhiani draws from some of his own experiences when writing the book. What do you think makes him qualified to insert his opinion on the topics in the book?

~~~

question 3

Lakhiani begins the book by helping readers understand the "culturescape" and how the world has shaped them. What does the term "culturescape" mean?

~~~

question 4

The book encourages readers to question the "collective rules of humanity." Give an example and why you think it should be questioned or challenged.

~~~

∼∼∼

question 5

The author teaches readers to be able to identify "Brules" because they limit creativity and growth. Why do you think the author refers to these as "brules"?

∼∼∼

~~~

question 6

The book says that readers will learn to "think like a hacker." What do you think Lakhiani means?

~~~

~~~

question 7

The author says that many of the beliefs that have been ingrained in you since childhood can keep you from succeeding. Give an example of a belief that you think may be holding you back, and tell why.

~~~

~~~

question 8

Lakhiani tells readers to update their daily system. What "daily system" in your life do you feel needs updating, and why?

~~~

question 9

According to Lakhiani, you should have two different visions in your mind at the same time. What do you think the author meant by this?

~~~

~~~

question 10

The author points out that the feeling of bliss you get after realizing a big goal is often fleeting. Give an example of a time in your life when you experienced "blissipline."

~~~

~~~

question 11

Lakhiani encourages readers to set goals that they are unwilling to compromise on. Why do you think this is important? Tell about a time when you set a goal that you knew you would not be able to compromise on.

~~~

question 12

Lakhiani teaches readers a process called "Six-Phase, in which they are required to do a 20-minute mind workout. Do you think this method would be effective? Why or why not?

~~~

question 13

The book is accompanied by an online experience. If you have had an opportunity to visit the site, what benefit do you think the website adds to the book?

~~~

~~~

question 14

Lakhiani presents over twenty new words to the English language. Which is your favorite, and why?

~~~

~~~

question 15

The author uses a learning model called Consciousness Engineering. What does consciousness engineering mean to you?

~~~

~~~

question 16

The book is a *New York Times* and *USA Today* Bestseller and is a Top Ten Non-Fiction title on Audible. Why do you think the book is seeing so much success?

~~~

question 17

A reviewer for *Publisher's Weekly* said that the anecdotes are occasionally "far away from the average reader. Do you agree with the reviewer? Why or why not?

~~~

question 18

Dave Asprey, founder of Bulletproof Coffee, said the book "will make you question everything you thought you knew about your life." What questions did you find yourself asking about your life as you read the book?

~~~

~~~

question 19

Jack Canfield, co-author of *Chicken Soup for the Soul,* said that the book should be required reading for high school seniors. What benefit do you think reading this book at a young age will have?

~~~

question 20

One reviewer suggested that the "constant name dropping got old." Do you agree with this reviewer? Why or why not?

~~~

Introducing the Author

Vishen Lakhiani, *New York Times* best-selling author of *The Code of the Extraordinary Mind*, was born and spent his childhood in Kuala Lumpur, Malaysia. He moved to the United States in 1995 to study Electrical Engineering and Computer Science at the University of Michigan.

While studying at the University of Michigan, he became a part of AIESEC, which is an organization run by students that nurtures young leaders who want to make a difference in the world. He was the Vice President of the United States team where his responsibility was to nominate and send AIESEC students overseas for internships.

After graduation, Lakhiani moved to New York where he went to work for a technology company. Because of the high level of stress in the job, he began meditating and learned a mindfulness program called The Silva Method. This inspired him to begin teaching classes.

Lakhiani is one of today's most influential people in the area of personal growth in the high tech educational industry. His company, Mindvalley, which specializes in designing learning experiences and creating digital platforms and apps, drives the education revolution. The curriculum produced by Mindvalley focuses on mindfulness, personal growth, well-being, productivity, and more. Lakhiani saw personal growth as a hobby at first, and he was surprised to see the success of Mindvalley, which has 500,000 students and two million subscribers. In 2012, his company was named as one of the coolest offices on the planet in a poll by *Inc.* magazine.

Not only is he the CEO of Mindvalley, Lakhiani is involved with other organizations related to learning and technology. He was the co-founder of Dealmates.com, which was recently acquired by iBuy Group. He is on the Innovation Board of a non-profit company called X Prize Foundation. He is on the Transformational Leadership Council, a support group for worldwide leaders.

Lakhiani now lives in Kuala Lumpur and often travels to New York City on business. In an interview, he said he had to get used to the Malaysian culture again—Malaysians aren't as outgoing and class is very important. He also noted that the business culture in Malaysia is different than in America.

Lakhiani is married with two young children. He says, in an interview with the BBC, that missing his wife and children is "the hardest part" about traveling from Malaysia to New York on a regular basis. He keeps in touch with his family through

Facebook and Skype. He also likes to record videos of New York for his son.

Fans of the author can connect with Lakhiani via social media—Facebook, Instagram, and Twitter. They can also find out more about Lakhiani and his work on one of his three websites—VishenLakhiana.com, MindvalleyAcademy.com, and Mindvalley.com.

Fireside Questions

"What would you do?"

Tip: These questions can be a fun exercise as it spurs creativity among the readers by allowing alternate scene endings and "if this was you" questions.

~~~

question 21

Lakhiani studied electrical engineering and computer science at the University of Michigan. How important would you say his education was to the success he is having?

~~~

~~~

question 22

Lakhiani lives in Kuala Lumpur and travels to New York quite often. How important do you think location is when running a company such as Mindvalley?

~~~

~~~

question 23

Lakhiani is on the Transformational Leadership Council, a support group for worldwide leaders. How do you think this association with worldwide leaders has helped him in writing his book?

~~~

~~~

question 24

Fans of the author can connect with Lakhiani via social media. How important do you think it is for authors to be available on social media platforms?

~~~

~~~

question 25

Lakhiani saw personal growth as a hobby at first, and he was surprised to see the success of Mindvalley. What do you think makes companies like Mindvalley so successful?

~~~

~~~

question 26

The author interviewed some of the world's most successful people, including Elon Musk and Richard Branson, among others. Who would you interview, and why?

~~~

question 27

The author says that he used the same style in his writing the book as he does in conversing with his friends over drinks. Would you have used the same conversational writing style or would you choose a more formal/business style, and why?

~~~

question 28

In the book, Lakhiani presents over twenty new words to the English language. What new word would you add, and why?

~~~

~~~

question 29

Lakhiani moved to the U.S. to study at the University of Michigan. How do you think his life and experiences would be different had he stayed in Malaysia?

~~~

~~~

question 30

Lakhiani travels back and forth from Kuala Lumpur to New York City for business purposes. Would you be willing to travel this much for your career? Why or why not?

~~~

Quiz Questions

"Ready to Announce the Winners?"

Tip: Create a leaderboard and track scores to see who gets the most correct answers. Winners required. Prizes optional.

~~~

quiz question 1

Lakhiani gives readers _____ rules to follow to live a more success life.

~~~

~~~

quiz question 2

_____ are what the author calls "bullshit rules."

~~~

~~~

quiz question 3

True or False: In the book, Readers will learn to think like a teacher."

~~~

~~~

quiz question 4

The book teaches readers how to better their lives by updating their daily _____.

~~~

~~~

quiz question 5

True or False: According to rule 6, you have to be able to visualize your present as well as your past.

~~~

~~~

quiz question 6

True or False: Lakhiani encourages readers to set goals that they are unwilling to compromise on—the author calls this being "unfuckwithable."

~~~

quiz question 7

Lakhiani teaches readers _____, a 20-minute daily workout for the mind.

~~~

~~~

quiz question 8

True or False: The author used the same style in his writing the book as he does in conversing with his friends over drinks.

~~~

~ ~ ~

quiz question 9

Lakhiani was born and raised in
_____.

~ ~ ~

~~~

quiz question 10

Lakhiani studied electrical engineering and computer science at _____.

~~~

quiz question 11

True or False: Lakhiani's company is called WealthyMinds.

~~~

quiz question 12

True or False: Lakhiani travels from Malaysia to New York City several times a year.

~~~

Quiz Answers

1. ten
2. brules
3. False; "think like a hacker"
4. systems
5. False; you have to be able to visualize your future as well as your present.
6. True
7. Six-Phase
8. True
9. Kuala Lumpur, Malaysia
10. University of Michigan
11. False; Mindvalley
12. True

Ways to Continue Your Reading

EVERY month, our team runs through a wide selection of books to pick the best titles for readers and reading groups, and promotes these titles to our thousands of readers – sometimes with free downloads, sale dates, and additional brochures.

If you have not yet read the original work or would like to read it again, get the book here.

Want to register yourself or a book group? It's free and takes 1-click.

Register here.

On the Next Page…

Please write us your reviews! Any length would be fine but we'd appreciate hearing you more! We'd be SO grateful.

Till next time,

BookHabits

"Loving Books is Actually a Habit"

CPSIA information can be obtained
at www.ICGtesting.com
Printed in the USA
BVHW071332011218
534523BV00002B/313/P